Adirondack
GHOSTS

ISBN 0-9700718-1-7

All photos taken by the author unless otherwise noted.

Book cover by Jo Butz, *Graphic Design Studio.*

Back cover graphic by *CatStuff.*

Printed on recycled paper by *Sheridan Books.*

Cover photo: *Buzz Point at Covewood Lodge on Big Moose Lake, Eagle Bay.*

CONTENTS

INTRODUCTION

There are mysteries in this world that cannot be explained and ghosts hover near the top of the list.

New York State's stunningly beautiful Adirondack Mountains are rich in natural resources and hold a wealth of history. Covering over 6 million acres, they also abound with mysterious beings that roam the region.

Adirondackers are fond of their phantoms and speak of them candidly. Spirits are clearly part of the culture of mountain life.

The area has had its share of murders, suicides, and untimely passings. We can only speculate as to what keeps the departed coming back to their Adirondack haunts. Anyone who has visited the North Country can readily understand the wraiths' reluctance to leave their earthly abode. Is their longing merely for the splendor of the region? My guess is that in some cases revenge and the unresolved circumstances of their death keep them here.

From the time Native Americans inhabited the region, through the French and Indian and Revolutionary Wars, up to this very minute, ghosts are "alive" in the Adirondack Mountains and making their presence known in a variety of annoying, helpful, playful, and terrifying ways.

In 1988 I had my own ghostly sighting at Big Moose Lake while staying at Covewood Lodge in Eagle Bay. *Unsolved Mysteries* reproduced the event and told the story of the 1906 murder of Grace Brown. The episode aired for the first time in January 1996.

Adirondack Ghosts begins with this personal account and proceeds to present a brief history of hauntings in the Great North Woods from the 17th century to the millennium.

Turn the pages and walk with the spirits that haunt the Adirondack Mountains of New York State.

Grace Brown left from this hotel for a fatal rowboat ride on Big Moose Lake in 1906.

BIG MOOSE LAKE
Eagle Bay

Does the ghost of Grace Brown still roam the environs of the deep-water cove where she was drowned in Big Moose Lake?

Her story lives thanks to Theodore Dreiser's famous novel, *An American Tragedy.* Hollywood cast Shelly Winters as the 19-year-old murdered woman in the movie production, *A Place in the Sun.* Montgomery Clift was nominated for an academy award for his performance, and Elizabeth Taylor, his co-star was only 17 years old.

Pregnant and unmarried, 19-year-old Grace Brown was murdered in 1906 by social climber Chester Gillette, the father of her unborn child. He was convicted and executed in the electric chair. Nearly 100 years ago, this was the "trial of the century."

In 1988 I saw what I believe was Grace Brown's ghost while vacationing at Covewood Lodge on Big Moose Lake in Eagle Bay.

While canoeing in a secluded cove of the lake the water in that area was noticeably dark and looked fathomless.

That same night I ventured out alone for a walk but quickly returned to the cottage for my friend to keep me company because my flashlight had stopped working and no way was I going out alone.

Big Moose Lake is remote and isolated and I was uncomfortable out in the dark without a light to guide me. All my batteries were fresh but this was the third incident of electronic shutdown – my camera flash and travel clock had also stopped working.

We sat out in the "Buzz Point" gazebo at the end of the peninsula on the lake chatting and listening to the loons. A white vapor idly floated up the lake from the cove we had explored earlier in the day. After a while we noticed the mist stop and hover in front of a stand of dark spruce trees.

Quite unexpectedly we realized that the cloud was taking shape. The form was clearly that of a woman! Her profile was distinct. I remember looking for her feet and noticed they trailed off in the haze. I wasn't frightened but did feel an incredible sadness emanating from the ghostly woman. It seemed as if she was looking for the families who had stayed at the resort.

We watched in awe until she dissipated.

The next morning the owner of Covewood let us tour the main lodge even though it was closed for the season. While perusing photos and other memorabilia we found an article about the drowning of Grace Brown in Punky Bay, the deepest part of the lake and the same spot from where the mist traveled from the night before.

We told our story to another friend who had worked at Covewood that summer and she had a tale of her own to tell.

One night she and her co-workers returned to the staff quarters after watching a movie at the main lodge. She went up the stairs to her room and froze as she reached to turn on the light – someone was in the room with her. She called out her friend's name. . . .

But her friend was still outside with two other lodge employees. When they heard her call they looked up at the window and witnessed a whitish illuminated female form linger for a moment and then *"whoosh"* disappear.

UNSOLVED MYSTERIES cast and crewmembers prepare to film a scene for the "Grace's Ghost" episode at Covewood Lodge.

As we shared our stories, we all realized we had experienced something extraordinary.

Does Grace Brown's ghost inhabit the woods and exert an energy drain that renders equipment temporarily out of order? My problems with my camera flash, clock and flashlight may have resulted from such a force.

The Adirondack tragedy is an integral part of American history and I felt these unusual events would make an interesting presentation on *Unsolved Mysteries*.

In May 1995 the show's talented crew recreated and videotaped the Adirondack's most famous murder and subsequent sightings of a spirit at Big Moose Lake.

"TJ," a former Covewood manager shared even more happenings.

One late afternoon a couple stopped by to see the main lodge as a possible site for their wedding reception. TJ invited them to look around on their own, but requested that they turn off all the lights in the building when they were through.

That evening as TJ was heading home he felt compelled to look back at the main lodge. Seeing that the lights had been left on, he shook in head in annoyance. TJ unlocked the lodge, turned the light switch off upstairs, and locked the door behind him. One more backward glance. The second floor windows glowed with light. He repeated the routine two more times and finally decided to give up, frustrated by the unseen trickster.

The *Unsolved Mysteries* episode of "Grace's Ghost" can still be seen in re-run on the *Lifetime* network.

JACKSON'S LOG HOME
Indian Lake

"I beheld what I wish never to behold again."

The above quote is an excerpt from the article "The Haunted House" published by the *Warrensburgh News* on February 29, 1880. It speaks to the horror witnessed by its author, known only by the initials "F.A.M."

On December 25, 1879 a group of hunters, trappers and guides were celebrating the holiday at Beriah Wilbur's Hotel in Indian Lake. The fierce winter wind howled outside, but inside the atmosphere was warm and convivial as the men sat around a roaring fire telling tales.

At the stroke of midnight, the conversation turned to ghosts. Storyteller "Old Print" taunted young F.A.M. into staying the night at the reputed haunted log home on the Jackson property two miles away. Not willing to appear cowardly, he accepted the dare.

Confronting the bitterly cold night, F.A.M. hiked through dense woods and huge snowdrifts that were challenge enough, but when he arrived at the deserted house the true test of bravery began.

Equipped with candles and matches from the hotel, he lit a tallow. The candle burned an eerie blue light casting strange shadows on the walls. He gathered up the few pieces of wood strewn about the room and started a fire. That also blazed an unusual bluish glow.

Poof! Suddenly all flames blew out. Not even an ember glowed from the hearth. The room seemed blacker than black.

This was too much for the lad to bear and as he groped for the door he felt a clammy face and heard a ghastly groan, a wailing cry, and chains dragging over the roof of the house. His hair stood on end as he broke into a cold sweat. He thought his pounding heart would beat out of his chest. Then he beheld what he wished never to behold again... .

In the corner a small phosphorus light grew bigger and brighter and a thin vapor formed into the shape of an old man. The cloudy figure circled the room and stopped in front of the terrified lad. As the apparition opened its mouth to speak, a stream of fire came out of the earthen floor. More ungodly groans and howling.

Once again, the room went black. F.A.M. ran from the horror filled house and made it back to the hotel where all were fast asleep. He spent a sleepless night mulling over his vision.

The next morning "Old Print" made good on his $5 bet, for F.A.M. had experienced what the old storyteller himself had seen and heard at the forsaken haunt.

And who is lingering at Jackson's log home? The consensus is that it's old Sabael the legendary trapper who some say was murdered in the house in 1805, and up until 1880, was still setting his "traps" there.

THE OLD PEDDLER
Indian Lake

Benjamin Butler arrived in Indian Lake with his crew of Canadian lumberjacks in the mid 1800s and set up his lumber camp at the foot of Peaked Mountain.

One day a peculiar old peddler pulled in to the camp sitting atop a dilapidated wagon. He was large and loathsome in appearance. His huge hands with pointy fingers and white disheveled hair were gross enough but his meanest feature was his red piercing eyes that glowered from his bewhiskered, course face.

By trade, peddlers were solitary men. Always on the move, close relationships were rarely developed. Traveling alone with desirable articles and the money they had to carry on their person made them vulnerable and furtive.

The old peddler emitted this attitude and made no eye contact with his potential customers, so the loggers felt he was hiding something and was out to rip them off. They found his appearance offensive and his suspicious manner even more so.

Inevitably, the peddler was murdered. His body, along with his horse and wagon were dumped in an old root cellar that was set ablaze to destroy any evidence.

Years later, Stephen Lamphere bought the old lumber camp and built a house on the property.

That's when the stories of the haunting began.

Late at night, Lamphere would hear someone enter the house and move about. Around midnight, footsteps were heard on the upper floor. Definite rapping was heard on a windowpane, and a woman's wail emanated from the cellar.

The scariest phenomenon of them all was the appearance of the unshorn peddler's face with long white hair trailing on the ground.

His specter was also seen riding behind his emaciated horse, and the racket made by the broken-down wagon was heard.

By 1900 Behr-Manning owned the estate and Willet Randall was hired as caretaker. He was duly warned of the strange goings-on.

Randall was quick to discover the sources of the "ghostly" activities.

A limb blowing against the roof was the culprit that caused the sound of tapping on the window. A sheep had wandered into the house and was walking around upstairs. An open end of a milk bottle facing the wind created the wail coming from the cellar.

Randall had an explanation for all – except one.

While entertaining guests, his friend's wife remained out on the porch. After awhile she went running into the house screaming and shaking from fright. She claimed to have seen the devil with a long white beard and blood red eyes. His long bony fingers reached out to grab her.

The men tried to comfort her suggesting it was only her imagination but the woman was certain and Randall's company abruptly left.

For thirty-seven years Randall lived in the house and had forgotten that the previous owner Lamphere had told him that one June evening during a full moon, he had heard the rattling of the peddler's cart coming up the road. His ghost eventually showed up at the house.

Yes, Randall had forgotten this story until one such June evening when he himself had an inexplicable rendezvous.

To quote the eloquent man directly from an interview printed in the *Indian Lake Bulletin*: *"I was sitting on the porch watching the deer feeding nearby and enjoying the chorus of crickets and the tree frog....Suddenly, the frog was still; the crickets were gone; a deer raised her head, ears thrown forward, then with a snort, bounded away. Silence brooded....Then, without further warning, I heard a rumbling sound of a running horse. I listened. It came closer. There was no mistake about it this time."*

Randall goes on to say how he heard the wagon wheels and the horse's hooves approaching. Then a crack of the whip and shouted profanities. A scream was heard and then he saw an indistinct form of a white bearded driver.

As Randall bolted from his chair in fright he heard the words, *"Watch out. I'm coming."* Then silence and the ghost vanished into thin air.

Despite this terror Randall remained an unbeliever. Are you?

RHINELANDER ESTATE
Elm Lake

In 1815 while struggling townsfolk built crude log homes, the prominent and wealthy Phillip Rhinelander, Jr., decided it was time to develop his family's long held landmass in Township Nine. Rhinelander had a vision of a thriving four cornered village; he imagined present day Speculator.

With the help of slaves and servants, he erected a mansion on the hillside and proceeded to clear his scenic three hundred acres on Elm Lake near Lake Pleasant.

The magnificent home featured large rooms, a center hall mahogany staircase and two huge fireplaces. The house was richly decorated with massive furniture and beautiful oil paintings. The kitchen boasted an enormous oven laid with clay bricks manufactured on the property.

A cut-stone terrace greeted visitors at the front door alongside a park Rhinelander had landscaped. Manicured lawns sloped to the lake, apple, plum and pear orchards, a vineyard, huge flower garden, and a one hundred-acre farm to feed the family and workers were part of the grand estate.

Stables and a carriage house were in the back along with the outhouses provided for the servants as well as a cemetery for the hired help to bury their dead.

Cows, horses, sheep and oxen grazed in the fields during the day and were housed in ample barns at night.

His estate was self-sufficient and a bustling community unto itself.

Rhinelander built a gristmill and a sawmill at the outlet of Lake Pleasant where the water falls and becomes the thunderous Sacandaga River.

Phillip had married the beautiful Mary Colden Hoffman and they had two children together. Their son was born first in 1815 and died 24 years later in Vienna. Mary gave birth to their daughter on April 7, 1818 on the estate.

After having developed his property, it was time for Phillip to make his mark in the realm of community affairs. His first political achievement was his election as assessor. Then he was appointed schools commissioner and Overseer of Highways, as well as inspector of elections.

Phillip loved his wife dearly but this model citizen had a dark side, he was an insanely jealous man. He kept poor Mary a virtual prisoner on the property.

Her letters to friends were confiscated and destroyed by Phillip. In fact a peddler who visited the house and spoke with Mrs. Rhinelander was found dead on the grounds of the estate. A servant who befriended the Mrs. was also found dead. Rumors abounded that Rhinelander ordered them murdered or that he did the deeds himself.

Mary died on September 7, 1818 the five-month anniversary of the birth of their daughter and her namesake. Some say Rhinelander had a hand in her untimely death suspected to be from poisoning.

Phillip, at first unwilling to let his precious Mary go, had a crypt built near the house with a majestic painted ceiling depicting angels and the heavens. He kept her body there until the spring when she was interred in New York City.

Rhinelander remained on his estate for the next five years, and was elected as Town Supervisor for two terms. Shortly after the last election, however, he became paralyzed and left Lake Pleasant to live in Manhattan. He passed away in 1830.

An Englishman named Thomas Wayne lived in the house for the next four years, but after that a caretaker saw to the needs of the house and the animals.

While sleeping in Mrs. Rhinelander's former bedroom a woman's audible sobs roused the worker. He awoke and saw a grief-stricken woman. As he reached out for her, she vanished into thin air.

Another workman heard rustling skirts, excited conversation and the sound of a woman combing her hair in that same room.

It became increasingly difficult to sleep anywhere in the house. The sound of a man in riding boots ascending the stairs was disturbing as well as the tugging away of the bedclothes from anyone trying to sleep.

Ghosts were sighted in the hall and one even disappeared into the boarded up fireplace in the drawing room. One day a large pumpkin came spinning down the center hall and smashed into the wall.

Isaac Page was employed as caretaker for awhile. The day their son died, their daughter was left behind at the house to do the necessary chores. While working alone, a bundle of candles used to illuminate the dwelling flew into the air. No body was there to cause this frightening anomaly.

For about fifty years, Mary Rhinelander's ghost haunted the Elm Lake house and even appeared during broad daylight to men working in the fields.

Even the ghost of the woman who used to wash Mary's clothes in the stream was seen near the water's edge. Eventually, all who worked at the estate made sure they vacated the grounds before dark.

After the house burned down in 1874, the appearances lessened, although sometimes apparitions are still seen roaming the remote ruins of the Rhinelander estate.

The forests have reclaimed the grounds of the once elegant manor and the International Paper Company now owns the land.

A friendly ghost has been seen at the Chapman Historical Museum

CHAPMAN HISTORICAL MUSEUM
348 Glen Street, Glens Falls

The Chapman Historical Museum in downtown Glens Falls exhibits regional history in a charming Victorian home once owned by Zopher DeLong, a local hardware merchant. No one wants to talk about ghosts there these days, but in the fall of 1988, former museum director, Kathy Allen gave an interview to the *Chronicle* and told them all about "Anna."

A psychic concluded that Anna was the DeLong's resident housekeeper in the 1800s. Allen says she saw the apparition when she looked out of her office window one day. She glimpsed a figure standing in the museum at the double door entrance of the hallway. A woman was leaning on the door handles and watching people outside. *"She had on a long pink dress with puffy sleeves, brown hair parted in the middle. She was very elegant looking. She vanished as I was looking at her,"* Allen said. *It wasn't scary at all....She was just casually standing there. It was a very logical experience."*

Another sighting was by a Chapman trustee who, when leaving the parking lot, glanced back towards the locked museum and saw someone with a long heavy sleeve push the curtain back and look out the window.

A visiting psychic perceived that Anna was happy to see the house being preserved in such good condition.

Abigail West's wraith has been seen floating up and down West Mountain.

WEST MOUNTAIN
West Mountain Road, Glens Falls

Strange noises are heard up on West Mountain and the eerie sounds are attributed to Abigail West. Poor Abigail was caught unawares one day while walking in a field at the base of the mountain. A horrific thunderstorm quickly developed and before she could find shelter she was struck by lightening and killed.

Abigail was buried on the site where she died, but her remains were moved to the Bay Road Cemetery. A further disturbance to her eternal rest was that her headstone was stolen sometime in the 1960s. (It has since been recovered and placed on her grave).

According to legend, during thunder and lightening storms, Abigail still haunts the mountain where she died Her specter has been seen wearing a blue dress and traveling up and down the crest. Another telltale sign of her presence is the scent of perfume pervades the air.

Years ago the West Mountain region was potato farmland. Today it is a charming residential community. Some people near the area where she died experience unexplainable incidents of doors slamming and sewing machines run when they're not turned on.

So, if you're in the vicinity of West Mountain and detect a delightful aroma in the atmosphere, it might be Abigail warning you of an impeding thunderstorm.

The A rail Restaurant has a playful and sometimes annoying spirit.

20

ANVIL RESTAURANT
67 Broadway, Fort Edward

The supernatural capers at the Anvil Restaurant did not deter Neal and Annette Orsini from purchasing the establishment from Dave McDougall in 1986. As McDougall's head chef, Orsini was used to the playful and sometimes annoying ghost-in-residence, Sam D. Turner. If his name sounds familiar, it's because it appears on the front of the building that was built on the outer walls of old Fort Lyman.

The location is dripping with history.

Fort Edward was the most important military post between Albany and the St. Lawrence River. The site was also known as the "Great Carry," or "Wahacoloosencoochaleva, " to put in Native American terms. Every expedition to Lake George and farther north paused here for a final check before setting off into the wilderness.

The Anvil Restaurant was originally a blacksmith shop built in the 1840s by Alexander Burke. The second floor of the building was a paint shop for wagons, carriages and sleighs. The vehicles moved up a ramp and through the double doors, still visible today. The upstairs walls are decorated with the practice drawings eventually transferred to the wagons.

The haunting began in 1973 when McDougall began to transform the old building into a bar and restaurant. He regularly heard crashes, someone walking in the upper room, and the heavy front door would sometimes open on its own. When he found over fifty whisky bottles in the building, he had a feeling that his enterprise would probably please the noisy ghost. McDougall opened on New Year's Eve and the phantom celebrated by banging pots and pans in the kitchen.

The Orsinis took over ten years later. When Neal installed a credit card machine that would telephonically transmit cardholder's information, the line went dead the next day. He discovered that the wires inside the wall were severed. *Severed*, not gnawed as if by a varmit. This happened three times until the pest grew tired of fighting progress he guesses.

One of the ghost's favorite tricks was to change the radio channel. Rock music was strictly forbidden in the cozy restaurant. Many times during any given evening all in attendance would hear garbled channels as the tuning knob was turned to, you guessed it, a rock station. *No body was seen at the radio.*

One night at closing, a waitress was bringing the plants inside from the outdoor patio. The phantom prankster locked the door behind her between trips.

Martha Bartholomew shared that while filling ketchup bottles in the kitchen she had the definite sense that someone was watching her. When she turned around to look, a bottle came flying off the shelf. Fortunately, she caught it before it could hit her.

There seems to be no reason for these happenings and the events are unpredictable as well.

Bar Manager, Cynthia Sawyer had her own adventures. As a new employee she was counting out her cash and felt uneasy. Suspecting her discomfit was due to the possibility of a robbery, she took the money upstairs. When she came down from finishing her task, the decorative chains were swinging back and forth. *"It wasn't as if someone had just walked by them and pushed them because they would have slowed down. These heavy one inch thick chains were MOVING and they were not slowing down."* Needless to say, Cynthia made a hasty retreat.

Just a few weeks ago, while she was in the lounge, a steak sauce and ketchup bottle crashed to the bar. A patron gaped in disbelief, but Cynthia is used to these strange and random occurrences.

But the most dramatic manifestation was when Cynthia and her crew saw a ghost appear right before their eyes. The specter was that of a man with a smaller than average build. He lingered in the kitchen doorway for a few moments, then faded away. The threesome was terrified and groped at each other to allay their fear.

When you go to the Anvil Restaurant in the village of Fort Edward, and I highly recommend that you do, be sure to examine the photo of Sam D. Turner that hangs there. You'll notice that he's a little smaller than an average size man.... . Oh, and by the way, the kitchen door was once the back door of the blacksmith shop.

The Jane McCrea House has a haunted reputation. Fact or fiction?

JANE McCREA HOUSE
Fort Edward

Jane McCrea was a seventeen-year-old woman engaged to a British officer in Burgoyne's Army. On July 29, 1777 a party of Native Americans was sent to escort her to her wedding ceremony. In the meantime, an opposing band of Native Americans captured her at the house where she was waiting. She was brutally killed and scalped - her red gold hair was a coveted prize.

The report of her gruesome death clamored along the Hudson River and through the mountains of Vermont, causing volunteers to assemble against the British as nothing else had done. Thus the sacrifice of Jane McCrea greatly contributed to the swift defeat and surrender of Burgoyne which helped end the struggle for American independence.

Her remains were moved three times before their final resting-place alongside Duncan Campbell in Fort Edward's Union Cemetery.

But is Jane McCrea truly at rest? Some individuals are in dispute.

Her former 1758 riverfront home is a lovely private residence. Some people who have lived in McCrea's house claim to have experienced unusual phenomena. For instance, when previous residents have left the house with all the lights turned off, when they arrived home, the lights were on. Is this just a memory lapse?

Footsteps have been heard in the attic and that light has also been known to turn itself on. When the attic is inspected for intruders, no one is found up there.

The present owners, Mary and Robert Russo, cannot confirm these oddities. In fact, they did hear the footsteps in the attic, but after they had the heating system serviced and the air was bled from the lines, the sound of footsteps stopped. One of their relatives swears there's a presence upstairs, however.

A "ghost" web site on the Internet states that in a certain closet the atmosphere is icy cold and sometimes disembodied screams emanate from the cabinet.

The Russos haven't heard any screams yet, but they've only been living there for four years. Mrs. Russo did say they when they first moved in she thought she may have heard someone going up the stairs, but that sound soon stopped.

I also spoke to George Kilmer who owned the house for many years. An undertaker by profession, he felt that if there were any ghosts in the house he'd certainly be one to know.

Jane McCrea has every right to haunt her environs after the cruelty and indignity she suffered both during and after death. In fact, probably not all her remains are buried. Reportedly her skull is the subject of archeological study.

When it comes to ghosts, there's a thin line between fact and fantasy, but the bottom line is *can we really be sure?*

OLD FORT HOUSE MUSEUM
29 South Broadway, Fort Edward

Situated on the banks of the Hudson River, the Old Fort House was built in 1772 and is one of the oldest frame structures in upstate New York.

Exhibits at the museum complex display photographs and furnishings from the mid 18th to early 20th century, and offer visitors a view into the daily life of a rural New York community.

The antique house, constructed from timbers taken from old Fort Edward built twenty years earlier during the French and Indian War, was both American and British headquarters during the Revolution.

Among the famous at the Old Fort House during the War for Independence were General Benedict Arnold, Colonel Henry Knox, and General John Burgoyne. In 1783 General George Washington dined there; his bill in his own handwriting is on display.

The house holds permanent unseen guests as well.

A troublesome door has been opening on its own for over one hundred years. Originally the explanation was that the vibration from the water going over the old Fort Edward dam caused the door to open. But the dam was destroyed in 1973 and the door continues its movement.

The Old Fort House has a ghost who likes to be kept in the dark.

It seems that the strange events started when the museum began conducting candlelight evenings at the house during Christmastime.

An electric candle placed on the window ledge in a small side room fell onto the floor. According to an interview given to the *Chronicle*, museum director and village historian Paul McCarty said: "*You'd think someone took their hand and knocked it off. I watched it. This happened three times to me, a couple times to another person who worked there. When it was taped down, then the bulb kept going out. It happened five or six times.*" McCarty said he changed the candles and bulbs but nothing would work.

Maybe the ghost is dismayed by electric lights or perhaps something of a dark and tragic nature occurred to the invisible occupant in that room.

The specter is believed to be Abby Rogers Fort. Abby and her husband Abram bought the home in 1839 and lived in it until the late 1860s.

The staff had no choice; during the Christmas candlelight tours that room remained in the dark.

More than one spirit frequents the abode however. Years ago a cupola sat atop the house and a man used to be seen standing in the dome.

A board member suggested that possibly three Native Americans and several children haunt the house.

The spirits cause no harm – their presence at times is just a bit unsettling.

The line between history and legend is often blurred as in the case of the Skene Manor.

THE SKENE MANOR
Whitehall

Whitehall's Gothic-style Skene Manor is the only castle in the Adirondacks. Constructed of native stone in 1872, this landmark structure earned a listing on the National Register of Historic Places in 1974 through the efforts of the Historic Society of Whitehall.

The unique dwelling overlooks the harbor and surrounding village, but this was not the first house to grace the mountainside. In 1756 Colonel Philip Skene was given an enormous land grant which stretched along Lake Champlain from Crown Point all the way south to Fort Ann in payment for his military service and loyalty to the British Crown.

The Colonel and his wife Catherine settled in the Whitehall area and named the town Skenesborough. Skene built a sawmill and began mining iron ore, thereby developing the town along the Hudson River.

But Skene's life began to crumble when his beloved Catherine became ill and died. He laid her body to rest in a beautifully carved pine coffin and sealed it in lead for the return trip to England.

The French and Indian War was raging and Skene was forced from his home. Aggressors desecrated Catherine's sarcophagus; the lead casing was hacked apart and used for gunshot. Her jewelry was pilfered from her corpse and her remains were buried carelessly in the garden.

The history of haunting began when soldiers guarding the property witnessed Catherine's full-skirted apparition. Her ephemeral form would appear for a few moments and then turn into a glowing ball of light. The sight was so strange and terrifying that every guard standing watch asked to be excused from his post.

After the war, Colonel Skene petitioned unsuccessfully to reclaim his mountainside property.

The next owner of the prime mountain site was New York State Supreme Court Judge Joseph Potter. Potter commissioned Irish and Italian craftsmen to build the four-story towered dwelling with the finest materials. The house was furnished in a grand Victorian manner with solid mahogany doors, parquet floors, and marble fireplaces. Rich tapestries adorned the massive windows, framing splendid views.

Ghostly myths developed over time. One was that Phillip had buried Catherine in the side of the mountain because as long as she was above ground he could continue to receive her dowry payments. Skene's tremendous fortune makes this tale improbable. Another fable is that because her jewels were taken off her corpse, Catherine's disembodied hand, sporting a large distinctive ring, floats about the mansion in revolt.

The Skene Manor has been a bed and breakfast, dinner theatre, and a restaurant. Some entrepreneurial owners have tried to capitalize on the legends. Potter ran a funeral business and left empty caskets in the basement. One proprietor placed one of these coffins behind the bar with a bejeweled hand hanging out of the box and built a fountain around it.

Anyone visiting the historic site these days doesn't need such tawdry sideshows to be impressed. The Skene Manor Preservation group has labored long, hard and lovingly to restore the magnificent structure. A palpable and beneficial spirit does seem to pervade the house.

No ghosts have been seen there since the 18th century when Catherine appeared in the garden. But then again, what about that wintry day when a cross-country skier noticed a woman waving wildly at the window. Fearing an emergency, the skier rushed to the manor and banged on the door. A workman answered her knocks and the skier inquired if everything was all right explaining what she had observed. At that moment a tremendous crash was heard upstairs. The pair investigated the noise and discovered a collapsed ceiling in the room where the worker was making repairs. Who was this woman at the window signaling her warning and saving the man from injury, or worse?

Though not directly a Skene Manor ghost story, this next one bears relation and begs telling.

Whitehall is the birthplace of the United States Navy and the town has erected a memorial to one of its favorite sons, William "Bill" Hart.

The battleship *USS Maine* blew up and sank in Havana harbor on February 15, 1898. A terrible tragedy, 260 sailors died in the blast. Sadly, Bill Hart was one of the casualties and the only Whitehall enlistee.

Coincidentally, Judge Potter's son was a Rear Admiral in the Navy and assigned to investigate the controversial explosion.

On the day the ship sank, and before news of the horrific accident had reached his homeland, Bill Hart's mother in her Meath County, Ireland home heard someone knocking. When she answered the door she was thrilled to see her Bill had come to visit. She ran to get her husband, but when they returned to the front door he was gone and no where to be found.

Only later did they come to realize that his spirit appeared to say a final good-bye.

Bill Hart's spirit appeared to his mother in Ireland on February 15, 1898, the day he died on the USS Maine. (Photo courtesy of Donald F. Hart.)

BRANT LAKE

Howard Hayes recalls a ghostly Halloween tale from his boyhood days in Brant Lake.

Near the top of Graphite Mountain stood a small schoolhouse overlooking Brant Lake. In the early 1900s, a newcomer purchased an old house near the school. The man lived alone and seemed a bit odd because he always wore black and was not sociable with his neighbors or townsfolk. In fact he was seldom seen in public except on infrequent occasions when he drove his wagon and two white horses along local roads. His eccentricities scared some local lads. They were afraid of him because they didn't understand him.

Halloween arrived and mischief was in the minds of three boys in particular. They were looking for trouble and found it when they spotted the stranger riding along the dark road.

As the man and his horses approached a sharp curve, the three leapt off the hillside in front of the horse's path. The frenzied animals raced down the road deaf to the driver's command to control them. They veered off the mountainside and plunged into the rocky gulch below.

The man and his horses died in the crash.

The dead man's property was taken over by his heirs and three years later a couple wanted to buy the small

35

house. The heirs duly warned the buyers that the house was haunted and suggested that they agree to live in the house for a year before settling the transaction. The purchasers agreed.

One uneventful year later, having seen no ghost, they formalized the deal. At 5:00 PM on the following day the newcomers heard a team and wagon approaching. When they looked down the road, they saw an apparition of two white horses pulling a wagon driven by a man wearing a black suit.

Terrified by the ghostly sighting, they sold the property within a month. The frightened owners persuaded the new purchasers to live in the house for a year before concluding the sale. The newcomers agreed.

Only after they signed the contract of sale did they also experience the phantom driver in black and his team. Fearful, they vacated the property and the house stood vacant thereafter.

When Howard was growing up his father showed him the deserted "ghost house." The structure was overgrown with brush and large trees. As an older man in his 60s he returned to that road while visiting graves in Horicon. The old house had vanished from the site at the fork in the road. It looked as if no one had ever lived there.

All the players in that long ago Halloween prank are now gone. But Howard Hayes likes to remind young people to be careful of their Halloween mischief. His cautionary tale warns that thoughtless acts can turn deadly and may have long lasting effects.

FORT TICONDEROGA

The last two weekends of October are reserved for the *Haunted Fort* happening. This annual event held by the Fort Ticonderoga Historical Society and Guild attracts visitors from across the country and has become an annual tradition. This ghoulish gala grew from the ghostly sightings experienced at this stronghold.

In the mid-1700s Fort Ticonderoga was the "key to a continent." The St. Lawrence and Hudson Rivers was a vital trade corridor between present-day Montreal and New York City.

Initially the site was a trading post called Fort Carillon after its French founder Phillipe de Carillon. Appropriately re-named *Ticonderoga*, meaning "the place between two rivers " in Native American tongue.

The British first conquered the French bastion and not long after, Ethan Allen and his Green Mountain Boys from Vermont, along with Benedict Arnold, stormed the fort on May 10, 1775. This surprise attack was the first successful act of aggression of the American Revolution.

George Washington visited the fort in July 1783. The museum contains Washingtonian memorabilia and even a relic of Martha's wedding dress. Presidents James Madison and Thomas Jefferson were there in July 1791.

The fortress lay in ruins for years. Many of the stones were taken by locals and used in the building of their own homes.

In 1908 the Pell family resurrected the historic dwelling, which sits atop a peninsula overlooking the Champlain Valley.

The bastion is a National Registered Historical Site, not-for-profit educational institution, and a museum holding the world's largest and most impressive cannon collection.

Fort Ticonderoga is also haunted.

On a perfect autumn afternoon I entered the iron gates and drove along the monument lined road. The deadwood of centuries old spruce hung heavy over the site where in 1777, over three thousand lost their lives in battle. The bunkers marking the French lines are still evident.

To honor the dead, Marquis de Montcalm erected a gigantic cross. Many sensitive visitors feel depressed at this spot where a replica red cross towers.

The historic fort rates a listing in Dennis William Hauck's *Haunted Places*. Hauck cites the ghostly appearance of one of the garrison's former commanders, General "Mad" Anthony Wayne and his sweetheart, Nancy Coates. Coates committed suicide by walking into the lake after Wayne left her for another woman.

My visit elicited quite a few other ghostly tales.

I first encountered lead interpreter John M. Rice and asked if he had ever experienced any hauntings.

John M. Rice, lead interpreter at Fort Ticonderoga, had many ghostly experiences to share.

"Oh yes, there's lots of them. One day many re-enactors were here at the fort. One was standing alone. I went over to introduce himself and poof, he was gone."

Another time while standing in the dining hall, Rice noticed a grayish mist and a soldier with blue turn-backs. (Turn-backs are large blue cuffs on a French soldier's uniform, similar to the one Rice wears while "on duty" at the fort.) Rice watched and witnessed the French soldier walk right through a door.

He also saw a window casement move of its own accord. *"I know it happened because I had to pick it up."* Rice also explained that most of the sightings occur on mist-laden days.

Standing in front of the "Ladies from Hell" diorama depicting a scene of Campbell's Royal Highland Regiment, I interviewed Ruth Fitzgerald. This octogenarian was featured in a cable television presentation about the fort's paranormal anomalies.

Fitzgerald shared that while living in a house on the ground's lower road, she was responsible for tending the King's Farm. One day she heard a horse galloping. Fearing one of the farm's horses was loose, she rushed out front only to feel a breeze on her face and see the dust stirred up from the stampeding phantom.

Another oddity she offered is the small ball of light that travels around the top floor of the barracks building. *"Several of us have seen it."*

A week before my visit, an Englishman reported that he had seen a soldier sitting in General William

Johnson's 18th century side chair from the officer's dining room.

Also on the barracks's top floor, the sound of someone walking is heard in the morning before the museum is open to visitors. *"They're more frequent now that the front wall is crumbling. The spirit seems to be upset that the wall hasn't been repaired yet,"* said Fitzgerald.

When I asked another interpreter, Bev O'Neil, if she had experienced anything out of the ordinary, she replied with: *"Of course there's the footsteps in the morning."*

O'Neil also told me the story of a young Native American girl who jumped to her death from a high wall rather than submit to an officer who wanted his way with her. Her specter has been seen walking along the shoreline.

O'Neil was born and raised in Ticonderoga and has been an employee of the fort for over five years. She shared that one morning at daybreak she heard the sound of drums. Remembering the re-enactors were scheduled at the fort to commemorate an important anniversary, she roused herself and got ready for work.

She mentioned to several of the visiting drummers how she had heard them practicing early that morning. They were surprised because they didn't start playing until after 8:00 AM.

Who was that playing at dawn's first light? Bev O'Neil feels she knows.

The employees I spoke with who had had supernatural experiences feel a special connection to the fort and its rich history.

No doubt, Fort Ticonderoga's most famous spectral legend is Duncan Campbell subject of Robert Louis Stevenson's *The Master of Ballantrae.*

Duncan Campbell harbored a man seeking refuge from the law claiming he had killed a man in self-defense. Duncan later learned that the man he safeguarded had killed his cousin Donald. Bereft with grief and torn apart by guilt, he was nevertheless a man of his word. Duncan kept his promise to the murderer and helped him escape.

This decision disturbed his deceased cousin who appeared to him in his dreams warning: *"Till we meet again, Duncan, at Ticonderoga."*

Now, "Ticonderoga" was not a word on everyone's lips in 18th century Scotland; Duncan's nightmares concerned and confused him.

As a member of His Royal Highness' Black Watch Brigade, Duncan was sent to the colonies and was stationed at Fort Carillon in the northeastern wilderness. Only when Duncan arrived at the front line did he learn the alternate name for the fort – *Ticonderoga.*

During battle, the apparition of his cousin Donald manifested and reminded him: *"At last we meet again Duncan, at Ticonderoga."* Duncan finally understood.

He died three days later and was buried near the fort. In the mid 19th century his remains were moved to Fort Edward and buried alongside Jane McCrea also a war casualty killed in 1758.

It is said that on rainy, windy nights, the two cousins can be seen walking the grounds of the fort.

In 1820 William Ferris Pell purchased the property and the existing ruins. He built a grand lakeside colonial mansion and called his estate the Pavilion.

One day as the patriarch was returning home after an extended absence, his son was so excited to see his father he set off a cannon to announce his arrival. Tragically, the cannon exploded and killed the boy.

Although the Pavilion is closed to the public, workers and passers by in boats on the lake have seen the curtains being pulled back as if someone inside is looking out the window. Some feel this phenomenon is master Pell's ghost still watching and waiting for his father.

John Rice told me that one day three clairvoyant women were enjoying their day at the popular tourist attraction. As a visiting fife and drum corps played a rousing call to arms, the women saw dozens of spirits appear in answer to the call. They were so upset at the sight they left in tears.

Rice shared that it's common for people to feel an inexplicable sadness or an uncontrollable urge to cry. *"Some can't even make it through the door,"* he said.

The graves of Jane McCrea and Duncan Campbell in Union Cemetery.

GENERAL HAMMOND'S HOUSE
Crown Point

This next story comes from Gil Barker a lifelong resident of Crown Point whose family history in the area predates the Civil War.

A most incredible incident took place in the former 19th century residence of Civil War General John Hammond before the house burned down in 1923.

One Halloween around 1896, Barker's mother, who was around six years old at the time, opened the French doors to the second-floor balcony and went outside to hang the American flag from the railing. In those days, *"Halloween was treated as a holiday just like the Fourth of July,"* said Barker in an interview with *The Post Star* in October 1993.

Satisfied with her task, she went back into the house and closed the doors behind her.

All of a sudden the wind blew up, there was a clap of thunder, the doors flew open and in tumbled a huge ball of lightening the size and color of a large pumpkin.

The fireball bounced down the hall past the incredulous girl and then rolled down two flights of stairs to the cellar where it fizzled out and left a circular scorch mark on the floor.

Barker's mother felt that balls of lightening such as this one may have been the basis for Irving's *Headless Horseman* tale and similar stories of headless riders.

Mabel Smith Douglass left her Lake Placid camp to pick leaves one day and was not seen again until thirty years later when her perfectly preserved body was discovered resting on a ledge under the water near Pulpit Rock.

PULPIT ROCK
Lake Placid

On September 15, 1963 two divers discovered a woman's body sixty feet from Pulpit Rock. At first they thought it was a mannequin, but when they grabbed the arm and it came off in their hands, they knew they had found a corpse.

An investigation ensued and quickly the woman was identified as Mabel Smith Douglass reported missing thirty years earlier.

Mabel Smith Douglass was no ordinary woman. Born in Jersey City to a successful merchant, she marries an equally prosperous businessman. Enough for most women of her generation, but Douglass has greater ambitions. She attends Barnard College in Manhattan and graduates in 1899 with a Phi Beta Kappa key.

Her goal in life is to found a woman's college, a companion college to Rutgers, the New Jersey State University. Douglass focuses on this objective until 1915 when she has to curtail her work due to frail health.

In 1916, her husband of thirteen years dies and she's left to raise two small children and run the family business.

Two years later, Douglass' dream is realized however, with the establishment of the New Jersey College for Women. She is appointed its first dean.

Her career flourishes for five years and she becomes a legendary figure at the school. She is *beyond* dedicated devoting countless hours to her vocation and the welfare of the young women. Sometimes she works late into the night and sleeps on a cot at the school.

On September 9, 1923 her triumphant career is marred with tragedy when her son William commits suicide by shooting himself in their home.

Numerous achievements follow the terrible loss. Douglass receives an honorary doctorate of laws the next year. Thanks in part to her efforts, beautiful Voorhees Chapel opens on campus. She's appointed to the New Jersey State Board of Education and in 1930 is the first woman to receive the Columbia University Medal for distinguished public service. In 1932 Russell Sage College presents her with an honorary doctorate degree and she is named *Officier d'Academie* by the French government for promoting French language education in the United States.

Inevitably, she suffers a nervous breakdown, takes a leave of absence from the college, and voluntarily commits herself to a private mental hospital in Westchester County, New York.

She remains in the hospital for one year and upon her release offers her resignation to the college and retreats to her Camp Onondaga on Lake Placid.

On the last day of her stay at her Adirondack refuge Douglass boards her St. Lawrence skiff supposedly to pick colorful fall leaves. But she rows across Lake Placid to Pulpit Rock directly across from her camp and notoriously the deepest part of the lake. Some say the water's depth in that area is fathomless.

Two workmen attested years later that they saw her on the lake standing in the skiff with a veil over her head. Then they claim she threw something into the water and she followed in after it overturning the boat. When they arrived at the boat and righted it, they noticed the oars were neatly tucked under the seats and found no trace of the woman.

Douglass' death was ruled an accident.

Thirty years later, *almost to the day*, her body is found. Due to the combination of the frigid water temperature and chemical salts in the water, her body's fatty tissues have virtually turned to soap. When her body was removed from its underwater resting-place and exposed to the air, the flesh fell away from the bone.

Her remains were interred in the family plot next to her husband and her son.

Strangely enough, Douglass' daughter Edith also suffered the death of her husband at an early age. Like her brother, Edith eventually committed suicide.

This tragic tale is exacerbated by stories of a female apparition hovering over the water near Pulpit Rock. The stories began when Douglass' body was raised from its frigid resting-place. On moonlit autumn evenings a nebulous female form has been seen. Who is haunting Pulpit Rock? Some say it's Mabel S. Douglass unable to rest since her peaceful sleep was broken in 1963.

Did Mabel Smith Douglass drown herself in the shadow of Whiteface Mountain or was it a tragic accident? Is she the female apparition seen hovering over the water near Pulpit Rock?

MRS. DELOS-BLODGETT
Lake Placid

"My mother had died and my father was living in Vermont, but spending so much time with me here in Lake Placid that I suggested he come live with me. I had found the perfect house on the lake." And so Lyn Witte began an extraordinary adventure.

Lyn Witte is the present manager of White Pine Camp, Calvin Coolidge's 1926 Summer White House, in Paul Smith's. But at one time she lived in a magnificent house on the shores of Lake Placid.

Lyn and her father were the fourth owners of the grand residence. Six bedrooms, six baths, huge entry hall with a central stairway, massive living room, eight fireplaces, servant quarters, large boathouse – these were just a few of the particulars of their new home. *"The minute I saw it, I knew I had to have it,"* was Lyn's first impression of the dwelling. Fortunately, they also "inherited" the caretaker, Victor LaFabe, a native of Lake Placid. Victor had been hired by the home's original owners and had known no other employment.

Delos-Bladgett, a wealthy financier, had the house built on Lake Placid as a summer home in the 1920s. His wife had a discerning eye for design and oversaw the creation of her new home both inside and out. She was a woman with style who knew what she wanted.

Lyn and her dad purchased the house fully furnished. *"There was furniture everywhere,"* she said.

Lyn is an avid decorator but in this space her urges to change the location of the furnishings were strong. For instance, a sofa in the boathouse seemed to belong in the living room; downstairs furniture fit better in the bedrooms. Her discerning eye went beyond good design; she claims that she felt *moved* to position particular pieces in certain spots.

Lyn and Victor worked together moving the objects around. But after awhile, Victor began to act apprehensive toward the new owner. Lyn sensed something was obviously wrong and she approached him about his odd behavior.

*"Oh nothing's wrong ma'am it's just that you're moving every piece of furniture **exactly** where Mrs. Delos-Bladgett had placed it when she lived here."*

Lyn was floored, though not deterred. She continued to redecorate replicating Mrs. Delos-Bladgett's style without exactly understanding why.

In fact, one day she felt compelled to go into the attic, and couldn't move fast enough to find whatever it was she was looking for. Drawn to a dark eave, there she discovered a magnificent mirror in the Chippendale style. Lyn practically ran down the attic stairs and directly to the first floor and placed the attractive mirror against a bare wall. To her amazement she detected the faint outline of the looking glass where it had hung sixty years before.

Lyn eventually learned that Mrs. Delos-Bladgett finished arranging her new home around Christmastime. The house was trimmed for the holidays and then she and her husband set off to Europe to celebrate. But Mrs. Delos-Blodgett would never see her beloved house again for she died in a car accident while traveling in Italy.

Lyn and her father had moved into their new home in September and she had completed making their new house into a home by following her inner prompting.

The holidays were fast approaching and the house needed to be decorated for Christmas.

One weekend she suggested to her friend Larry that they put up the tree. Well, not *the* Christmas tree - Lyn felt that they needed *eight*. With much effort they completed trimming the trees and at last Lyn felt her work was done. One two-story beauty in the entry hall was their *pièce de résistance*.

When Victor returned on Monday, Lyn couldn't wait to show off her festive creations. He was astonished and just shook his head in wonder. *"Mrs. Delos-Blodgett also put up **eight** trees. . .in exactly the same places you have them."*

From that moment on, Lyn never again felt an unseen hand directing her decorating scheme. To this day, she is convinced that the work she did in the house was to the satisfaction of its original designer and woman of the house Mrs. Delos-Blodgett.

Pete Harris stands at the top of the staircase in Knollwood Cottage where Preston Bickford's ghostly image appears on some photographs.

WHITEFACE CLUB
Whiteface Inn Road, Lake Placid

Nestled on the southwest cove of Lake Placid, the Whiteface Club began in 1888 as the Whiteface Inn. At that time, the Adirondack region was reputed for its balsam scented fresh air, thought to cure tuberculosis. Under the circumstances, the grand hotel flourished.

But disaster struck in 1908 when the inn was burned. The Bickford Family, who worked for the company as on-site caretakers and built the original edifice, rebuilt the lodge. Another inferno claimed the structure in 1917 and the Bickfords were still there to rebuild the inn. Yet a third conflagration claimed the inn and this time the structure was rebuilt by the Bickfords and soon cottages, convention hall, and an 18-hole golf course were added.

The Bickford Family was an institution at the property and their caretaking tradition extended to the next generation of five sons who grew up on the property and witnessed the development of the Whiteface Inn into a sophisticated and luxurious resort.

One son in particular was devotedly attached to the parcel of prime real estate and all the dwellings that his family had so painstakingly constructed and maintained. Preston Bickford had an unbelievable love for the place.

Preston spent his entire life, with the exception of the war years, working for the Whiteface Inn Company. He had his hand in everything and eventually became head plumber. But for Preston, there was a down side to working there.

The winds of change were blowing and in the 1980s when the main lodge was demolished to make way for modern condominiums, Preston stood on a hill leaning against his 1953 Willy's Jeep for support, and sobbed as the edifice crumbled.

Preston hated change.

In fact he was so resistant to change, and as a result of a misunderstanding of his retirement benefits, he sat on the edge on his bed, shot himself in the head, and died about a week later. That's when the unexplainable events began to occur at the Whiteface Club.

Jim Patterson was Preston's apprentice, and his best friend. Now that Pres was gone, Jim was the plumber in charge. Their relationship was so close that Jim feels Preston's spirit continues to help him from beyond the grave. When Jim has a problem running a new pipe, he'll stop what he's doing, look at it and feel a telepathic suggestion from his departed friend. When he looks at the project again, he'll see the job in a new configuration that makes perfect sense

But Preston's presence is not always so helpful. One morning when Jim went to turn on the heating system in the lower level of Convention Hall, where Preston had spent most of his time working, water was seeping through the ceiling.

The source of the leakage was difficult to trace but was ultimately found under the stage where a ¾" plug had been removed from the pipe. Who could have possibly dislodged the plug? The front of the stage platform had to be dismantled in order for Jim to crawl twenty-five feet under the landing to repair the leak. And where was the missing cap?

After he made the repair, Jim found the errant cap sitting on the windowsill above the stage. There could only be one explanation. Jim was certain that Preston's phantom had a hand in the destructive prank.

The manager on duty at the resort stays overnight on the grounds in the event of an emergency. Pete Harris, maintenance manager, had his turn to stand watch one memorable night.

He made his rounds to ensure everything was secure, then settled into his cabana room across from the public men's room. That's when he heard one of the urinals flush. He *"didn't even get out of bed. Well, yes I did, only to make sure the door was locked. My feet went cold."*

Another night during an inspection of the grounds, Pete saw that a light had been left on in one of the cottages. To his astonishment he discovered that the light was emanating from *behind* the refrigerator. To turn off the light, Pete had to pull the appliance out in order to remove the light bulb from the fixture in the alcove.

During renovations, evidence of Preston's handiwork was found in nearly every building. His signature and date of the labor were discovered written on the wood and walls.

Even the ladies' restroom was not off limits when it came to otherworldly goings on. A female employee was always accusing others of placing a chair behind the door in the lounge. She became so upset over the invasive and pervasive incidents that she finally quit her job. Assuredly no one (in the flesh) who was working there was to blame.

In the dining area, kids footsteps have been heard running across the floor. Could this be Preston and his brothers recreating their boyhood play? (Another brother also committed suicide). The large swinging kitchen doors have been seen moving back and forth as if being pushed by unseen hands.

A photograph taken in the Knollwood Cottage clearly shows a shadowy presence on the stairs. All who saw the image felt it was Preston.

During the summer of 1999 Preston's wife passed on. At the funeral, one of their children said, *"Guess Pop will leave you alone now"*

Actually since then, nothing unexplainable has happened. Well not unless you consider the fact that the sprinkler system went off this winter for no explainable reason flooding the entire Convention Hall building and causing $44,000.00 in damage.

Hopefully, this is Preston's last revenge.

Convention Hall at the Whiteface Club, haunt of a former employee.

A ghost who needs his morning coffee has visited Stevenson Memorial Cottage.

STEVENSON MEMORIAL COTTAGE
11 Stevenson Lane, Saranac Lake

For health reasons Robert Louis Stevenson spent the 1877-1878 winter at Baker's Cottage in Saranac Lake. Even though his good friend William Henley wrote of Stevenson: *"A spirit intense and rare,"* it is not the spirit of Stevenson that pervades the cottage.

According to curator Mike Delahant's grandmother, *"We're not the only ones living here."* The caretakers of the museum feel a palpable sadness and attribute the impression to Mrs. Baker. The Bakers lived into their eighties but were pre-deceased by their five children.

But the real ghost made his presence known to Mike and is believed to be that of "Old Quizzey." Mr. Quizell was a real character in Saranac Lake and best remembered for the zoo he established next to his live bait shop in town.

Old Quizzey had lived next door to the Baker cottage and when Mike needed a coffeepot because his had broken, he went to his neighbor's to see if they had an extra one. The present residents had one of Old Quizzey's that Mike could borrow.

Mike used the old aluminum percolator until he bought a new one. Quizzey's remained on the stove forgotten. One day as Mike walked through the kitchen, the pot flew off the stove, onto the table and then onto the floor. He guesses Old Quizzey wanted his pot back.

61

A bronze statue was erected in 1921 in Lake George's Battlefield Park to commemorate the role of Native Americans in the area's early history.

THE LEGEND OF THE SACRIFICIAL STONE

A large Indian Village once existed on Mohican Point. A female prisoner was brought to the village and held for ransom. The beautiful young woman immediately caught the eye, and heart, of the Chief's son, a brave young warrior and pride of the Mohican nation.

His affections angered the old women of the tribe who had already selected a Mohican maiden for him. Secretly, they decided that she must be killed.

The Chief's son left camp to lead a hunting party into the Adirondack wilderness. The old tribe women saw his absence as an opportunity. They dragged the maiden from her teepee to the center of their village and bound her to a pole. Their intention was to burn her at the stake. As the fire rose, a mysterious spirit appeared out of nowhere and diffused the devouring flames.

The spirit freed the maiden and transported her to a large boulder in the middle of a field and together they leapt from the stone flying high over the hills. The lovely maiden was never seen again.

Nor was the handsome young chieftain. He had disappeared from the hunting party the first night.

Every autumn a young warrior was found slain lying across the rock from which the couple had sprung out over the hills. They tribe believed that the Great Spirit had decreed that for every hair of the maiden's head seared by fire, a Mohican brave had to be sacrificed.

AN ADIRONDACK STORY ABOUT AN OLD CABIN MANY CENTURIES AGO
Rainbow Lake

Spring was a memory. The strawberries had passed their season and it was well into the depths of a warm summer when other plants reached fruition. Various medicine plants were ready to be respectfully harvested. It was at this time that a small family of Kanienkehake (People of the Flint/Mohawk) came into the mountains. The family was composed of a father, mother, young son, and grandfather. The mountains that they were traveling within are known as "Tsonontiskowa," in the Mohawk language, and in later years they were also known as the Adirondack Mountains. Untold generations of Mohawks have been among these mountains, and this little family was continuing that tradition, which continues to this day.

As late afternoon passed the father decided it was time to make a camp for the night. He chose a site near the end of a lake (some say it was Rainbow Lake). As the elders were preparing the camp, the young boy explored along the Lake's edge. He saw something that looked unusual reflecting from the other side of the lake, and he brought his parents' attention to it. They agreed, after peering at the image for a while, that it was the man-made angular shape of a roof. The roof of a bark house. They decided that it would make sense to go to that already prepared structure instead of creating a camp from scratch, so they traveled around the lake's end, and approached the bark house.

The bar house wasn't a big one like those in the village, which sometimes reached over one hundred feet. There were cobwebs within it, and evidence that porcupines and raccoons had spent time there too. This was easily cleaned up. They noted that at the end of the barkhouse there was a loft with an accessible log ladder. The father and son went up the ladder to investigate. In a dark corner near the far edge of the loft there was a squarish container made of bark. Curiously, they opened it, and were startled by the contents. Within the container was an old skeleton. The bones were bundled, and the lifeless eye-socketed skull was turned slightly to one side. The cover to the small bark casket was respectfully returned, then the two descended the ladder informing the others of the discovery. It was decided to simply leave it alone. The bones had been there for many years. The family continued to prepare for their evening without further thought of the loft's bundle.

It was decided that the grandfather would sleep on the bunk one side of the cabin, and the mother, father and young boy would sleep on the bunk on the opposite side. Between them was the fire pit, and as the fire dwindled the young boy was instantly asleep. The elders were soon to follow into sleep as the dying fire's shadows lengthened.

Some time later, the father was awakened by a gnawing sound. He thought immediately of the evidence of porcupine and assumed that's what it was. However, it sounded a little different. He reached up from his bunk and placed another piece of wood on the dying embers within the fire pit. Soon, the flames ignited the dry wood casting light into the cabin's interior. The father looked about the cabin; then he looked across the fire to the grandfather, and the sight struck shivering fear in his heart. The old man was apparently dead, and upon the lower part of his legs sat a skeleton! The movements of the skeleton were swift, and the eye-sockets were not empty for within them glowed fierce red embers. The teeth and chin were covered with stains of fresh blood; apparently it had been consuming the corpse of the old man. . .starting at the feet. Occasionally, the bloody skull would turn quickly to look with ember-eyes across the fire to the bunk where the rest of the family was. The father felt that this quick glance was directed toward the next items on the skeleton's menu.

Quietly the father woke the mother and the young boy. They too saw the skeleton, and a plan was hastily devised. When the fire went down again, the father added another piece of wood to it, and as the light increased the young boy got out of the bunk and said, "Father, I'm thirsty. . .I'm going down to the lake to get a drink." As he cautiously walked toward the door, he added, "I'll be right back." The skeleton watched the boy's movements until he left the barkhouse, but did not leave its perch on the old man's body. Then, it returned to its "feast," and by this time the legs were gone, and it was beginning to consume the upper torso.

Again, the fire darkened to embers and the father added more wood, resulting in light. The old man's body was eaten almost to mid-chest. This time the mother got up and said, "Husband, that boy is taking too long." She added, "I'm thirsty too. . .I'll get a drink and find out what's keeping him." Again, the skeleton watched as the woman left, then it continued its gruesome meal.

The darkened barkhouse was again bathed in light from the added wood to the embers in the firepit, and the father looked across the fire and saw that there wasn't much left to the grandfather. Only his shoulders and his head remained, and the skeleton continued to eat ravenously. "I'm going to check on those two, Grandfather," said the father toward the opposite bunk. "They're taking much too long. . .I'll be right back with them."

When he got a distance beyond the barkhouse, the father broke into a run. The mother and son had done the same previously, and were on their way back to the village in the valley from whence they had come the day before. Soon, the father's powerful strides brought him upon their heels, and he urged them to run faster. To the east there was a slight glow in the sky announcing the morning's sunrise. They ran, and ran. At one point, they were stopped dead in their tracks as they heard an ungodly wail coming from behind them. It started low, and reached a screaming crescendo that made the hair stand up on their necks. They continued to run, and at one point the father glanced back, and coming over a ridge that they had passed previously he saw the skeleton. It too was running, and it was taking inhumanly long strides that were the width of a barkhouse. There was no way that they could outrun this entity.

The sun, with piercing brilliance, suddenly broke over the horizon. The bounding skeleton moaned a painful scream, as it shuddered angrily to a stop. It peered toward its intended victims, then screamed into the graying sky. The skeleton turned and ran with great bounding strides back up the trail toward the bark cabin and out of sight. The family continued their flight toward the village and this time the only sound was their labored breathing as they ran.

When the trio reached the village, the people gathered to the shouts of their arrival. The father, the mother and the son told the story of their night escape. The men in the village gathered their weapons, and the father led them back up the trail toward the old bark cabin. Upon arrival at the site, some of the men encircled the cabin, as the father and the others entered it. The family's few belongings were where they had left them. Within the warm firepit lay the fresh almost white ash giving evidence of the firepit's recent use. On one bunk there remained only dark reddish bloodstains. There was nothing left of the grandfather's body.

Cautiously, with war clubs at the ready, the father and the two others went up the log ladder to the loft.

The bark coffin appeared untouched. The lid was lifted, and within were the bundled bones with the skull still turned with its lifeless eye-sockets to one side. However, there was a difference. The old and yellowed teeth were coated with stains of recent blood. The coffin cover was lowered; the men descended from the loft, and left the cabin. Dry brush and wood was put against the cabin on all sides. The cabin remained encircled by the men with war clubs raised and bowstrings were drawn taunt with readied arrows. Quickly, bowdrill fires were created and the flames were applied to the sides of the cabin. The old dry bark, brush and wood quickly ignited raising flames and sparks a great distance toward the sky. Scorching heat made the men step back a small bit, but their vigilance remained.

With a sudden "whooshing-pop," an explosion occurred within the burning house. The explosion was accompanied by the scattering of burning fragments and sparks rising above the pyre. Just as abruptly, from within the cabin's inferno, a white rabbit with glowing red eyes bounded out. The swift arrows and powerful swings of the clubs could not match the speed and agility of the rabbit. It bounded among the men, through their legs, then in an unmatched speed it streaked into the nearby forest. . .never to be seen again.

John Fadden
Six Nations Indian Museum
Onchiota, Adirondacks
July 31, 1997

From ghoulies and ghosties,

And long leggity beasties,

And things that go

bump in the night,

Good Lord, deliver us.

- Scottish Prayer

ACKNOWLEDGEMENTS

In pursuit of Adirondack ghost stories, I encountered many helpful individuals who must be thanked.

Peg Masters, Director, Township of Webb Historical Association, Old Forge.

In Indian Lake: Bill Zullo, Village Historian and Owner/Manager, 1870 Bed and Breakfast; Mabel and John Fish; and "Flossie" from the Indian Lake Chamber of Commerce.

Glens Falls: Marie Gaulin, Librarian, *The Post-Star;* Marilyn J. Van Dyke, Ph.D., President, Warren County Historical Society; Andrea Herman and Bill Martin, Crandall Public Library.

In Fort Edward: Neal Orsini, Martha Bartholomew, and Cynthia Sawyer from the Anvil Restaurant, and Dave McDougall; George Kilmer, Kilmer Funeral Home; and Mary Russo.

Donald F. Hart and Dottie Hart, Skene Manor Preservation Group, Whitehall.

Ruth Fitzgerald, Bev O'Neil, and John M. Rice, Fort Ticonderoga.

Betty Jean Morehouse, Vice President, Horicon Museum, Brant Lake.

Lyn Witte, White Pine Camp, Paul Smith's.

Pete Harris, Jim Patterson, and Joe Conto, Whiteface Club, Lake Placid.

Karla and Mike Delahant, Curators, Stevenson Memorial Cottage, Saranac Lake.

John Fadden, Director, Six Nations Indian Museum, Onchiota.

Thank you all for your time and contributions.

The Anvil Restaurant in historic Fort Edward.
(Sketch courtesy of Neal Orsini; artist unknown.)

BIBLIOGRAPHY

Aber, Ted and King, Stella, *The History of Hamilton County*. Great Wilderness Books, Lake Pleasant, NY; 1965.

_____, *Tales from an Adirondack County*. Prospect Books, Prospect, NY; 1978.

F.A.M., "The Haunted House." *Warrensburgh News*, Warrensburgh, NY; February 19, 1880.

Hauck, Dennis William, *Haunted Places*. Penguin Books, New York, NY; 1996.

James, Jeff, "Almanac: Reports of Local Ghosts." *The Chronicle*, Lone Oak Publishing Co., Inc., Glens Falls, NY; October 28 - November 12, 1988.

Miller, Joyce, Compilation of information regarding Abigail West. Crandall Library, Glens Falls, NY; 12/17/54.

Murray, Neil, "Haunted Houses." *The Post-Star*, Glens Falls Newspapers, Glens Falls, NY; 10/31/93.

Ortloff, George Christian, *A Lady in the Lake*. With Pipe and Book Publishers, Lake Placid, NY; 1985.

Order Form

BLACK CAT PRESS
Post Office Box 1218
Forked River, NJ 08731
E-mail: llmacken@hotmail.com

Please send _____ copies of *Adirondack Ghosts*

Please send _____ copies of *Haunted History of Staten Island*

To:

_____

_____

_____

_____

Price: $7.95 each

Sales Tax: New Jersey orders please include 6% sales tax.

Shipping/Handling: $2.50 for 1 book, $1.00 for each
additional book.
Please remit in check or money order payable to:

BLACK CAT PRESS

Total amount enclosed $ _____.

Quantity discounts are available on bulk purchases of
this book. For information, please contact the publisher.